I0418588

THE
LOST
POEMS

ALSO BY TIKIA CLEMENT

Eye Am Poetry

Testifying My Way

Shades of Emotions

Lift Up Your Voice

THE
LOST
POEMS

TIKIA CLEMENT

The Lost Poems
Copyright © 2025 by **Tikia Clement.** All Rights Reserved.
Published by Dream Elite Strive for Xcellence Publishing

All rights reserved. No part of this publication may be reproduced, distributed, or transmitted in any form, by any means, including photocopying, recording, or other electronic or mechanical methods, without the prior written permission of the publisher, except in case of brief quotations embodied in critical reviews and certain other noncommercial uses permitted by copyright law. For permission requests, write to the publisher, addressed "Attention: Permissions Coordinator," at the email below.

dreamelitestriveforxcellence@gmail.com

Title: The Lost Poems/Tikia Clement

ISBN: **979-8-9908227-4-0 (paperback)**

Any references to historical events, real people, or real places are used fictitiously. Names, characters, and places are products of the author's imagination.

Published and Printed in the USA

First Printing Edition **2025.**
Publisher: **Dream Elite Strive for Xcellence Publishing**

CONTENTS

Wake Up

wake up, brothers
wake up, sisters
disaster is near
fear is in the air
destruction is upon us
death is the reality
the corrupt do not care about casualties
do not allow man to dictate your reality
wake up before it's too late
time is running out
alliances have been formed
hate is the new norm
weather storms
when there is sleet, hail, earthquakes, tornadoes, or hurricanes,
call on His name
have faith and endure 'til the end
carnal living will lead to a spiritual ending
decisions, decisions
these decisions have life altering consequences
the stakes will always be high when you are navigating through
life
trust in the Most High
choose to be on the righteous side of His-Story
pride will have you starving for knowledge and thirsting for the
truth
turn back to the Most High
time is not on our side

Dry Bones

the bones are dry
the word is water, we rise
remember who you are beautiful, blessed tribe

Activation

Destination
Activation
Call every nation
Tell them we are here
Let them know as one, we are feared
We are no longer enslaved
mentally, physically, or spiritually

Destination
Activation
Call our kings
Our men are strong
Our men were born to lead
Our men represent His image
Our men are blessed and ordained to be kings

Destination
Activation
Call our queens
Our women possess a natural beauty
Our women are elegant and should hold their heads high
Our women represent strength and wisdom
Our women are queens and the key to his peace

Destination
Activation
Call on the tribe
Wake up family
Organize and unify our community
Pray for spiritual peace
Move with a sense of purpose

Unity, Unity,
Tell all the communities

Community

We, as people, need to unite
The community is fractured but can be repaired
Restored back to good health
Restored back to its wealth
Restored back to its blessings
Restored back to its identity
Community or tribe,
We've got to unite to survive
Love your brother as yourself
Hug your sister with love and care
The restored Black family is what the world fears

What the World Fears

Sis, tell your brother it is always LOVE
Bro, tell your sister she is enough and worthy of your LOVE
Protect each other
Go to war for one another
Us as one — the world fears
Be proud of who you are
Move with grace
We represent His love
It is time to lock arms
Bring to life our community, what the world fears

Those Days

This moment reminds me of back in the day when my people were in shackles and enslaved. Who would think we would make it this far. Labeled with scars mapping out the pain. Some fought to be free while burying our youth in graves. We've been through more than most can comprehend, and yet still we rise. We've learned how to survive. But something is holding us back, the soil speaks of the injustice. The banks reek of funded genocide. The rivers and lakes scream thriving Black communities, but now it's hidden history. We were labeled as a mystery. They miseducated us on our history. Some called it the foundation of self-hate. Some claim it was to make America great. We call it genocide. They want my people to comply, so they can continue to prosper on stolen land. They have fallen from grace, a disgrace to the world. The last will be first, and the first will be last. We were once royalty. We will reclaim our status on earth.

Different World

My heart hurts for our youth
How can they live an ordinary life?
They can no longer run outside and play in peace
The risk of someone doing harm to the community is at an all-time high
The dangers of going outside have increased
No more going to the store to buy snacks, demonic beings have hindered that
Youth can no longer go to school and learn in peace
Bullying has become the norm
If you do not conform, someone will treat you as if you do not belong
Sometimes our youth are living in a silent war zone, when all they want is to make it home
We are living in dangerous times
The world is consumed with hate
So many of our youth have disappeared
Where are they?
The authorities do not care
Families go through hell to get the authorities' attention
No national coverage when our children vanish
How can humans disappear?
So many are missing
So many do not care
Families beg for equality in the form of fair, accurate, and thorough investigations
They are instructed to wait
Time is not on our side
Valuable time slowly passes without any updates
Sadly, some families never receive any updates
No Amber Alerts for the poor
All lives are supposed to matter, but when you do not fit the description or have endless funds nothing will be done

Different Worlds

Our backgrounds are different, but we are relatable.
Sometimes, our pain is identical but don't tear me down when I oppose you.
Do not belittle me because I am genuine.
Stop judging me based on the standards given by man.
I'm not your child, so don't communicate with me as if you birthed me.
Some think words do not hurt, but words matter.
Sometimes those words leave many emotionally imbalanced, creating resentment and further unfavorable encounters.
Sometimes, words leave people feeling empty.
Sometimes, words lead people astray.
So do not tell me words, do not hurt.
Words may impact people in a way least expected.
Don't think what you say is meaningless or insignificant.
These interactions are invaluable but may leave many scarred.
I'm not trying to be difficult, but the world has broken me, leaving no room for happy days.
I carry pain from person to person leaving pieces of brokenness.
I cannot admit that I'm damaged, but I am not your doormat.
So, when you interact with me don't think that you can take advantage of me.
This is not the streets.
So, I carry myself like this is my last lifeline.
Don't threaten my livelihood acting like you're too good.
Don't look down upon me, as if you are superior to me.
This life isn't mine, but my character belongs to me.
I won't allow you to assassinate my character because you want to live.
If we cannot coexist, who becomes the casualty of cattiness, miscommunication, jealousy, envy, greed and hate.
I just want to be great, but you want to take my place.

Young Man

young man,
take a moment to think about your future
stop acting on impulse
be responsible
protect your brother
see value in each other
understand taking a life does not make you a man
be forward-thinking
realize the impact of self-hate
your selfish acts leave,
>   *parents left to mourn*
>   *children left fatherless*
>   *families torn*

life does not go on
taking a life does not solve your problems
it creates a lifetime of problems
understand in time you will be next to fall
another lifeless body lying on the ground
love yourself enough to stop the cycle of,
>   *broken homes*
>   *addiction*
>   *self-destruction*

recognize your current way of living is a form of genocide
put the guns down
retire the signs
reunite with your brother
repair and rebuild your community
it's time for unity

Mirrors

The resemblance is remarkable. Your eyes do not lie. Fighting these demons, everything happens for a reason. What do you see? The reflection is identical. It's just another day of you committing acts of war against the people who resemble you. He's a carbon copy of you. As you're searching for answers, the questions keep coming. Now you're running in circles. Is it okay to hurt him? He's 5'5, and you're 6'2. He's your brother, just repackaged in a different shade and different size. He's a precious creation, but you're conditioned to think he's crossed enemy lines. His energy is the perfect match. Some call it exact. It's a visual representation of you. Mirrors do not lie. Are you willing to swallow your pride or commit another crime? Ego is your downfall. Do not allow those demons to materialize your thoughts into anger. Look in the mirror and say, "He's not just another gang banger riding for enemies." Because if you settle this score, you can't come back for more. Close the door on public enemy #1. Guns don't make you invincible. There's nothing new under the sun. So, you may defeat him — maybe even won. But what about the loss of your soul? Your vision is blurry, and you're seeing red. Could it be that you're dead? Open your heart to being spiritually fed. A malnourished soul has you at risk of being spiritually dead. You're intellectually foolish. Open your ears and hear these words: You ain't gotta flip bricks by selling out your community, pushing poison to your people. Understand that with the Most High is where the real gangsters reside. Look me in the eyes and repeat these words:

Grace, Anointed, Nurturer, Glory, Salvation, Truth, Eternity, Righteous, Sabbath

It's time to choose the Most High.

Danger

Warning, warning
Trials and tribulations are near
So many are unprepared for the storm of a lifetime
Crime rates are higher than normal
Hunger is on the rise
Children cry
Homelessness is the new norm
Many lives have been sacrificed for the rich, but at what cost?
Leaders cannot justify their actions but pass bills against the will
of the people
Legalized crimes
Overtaxed is legal robbery
A nation unprepared, is a nation set up for destruction
People are unaware
Some do not have the eyes to see
Others do not have the ears to hear
Many move without a care
Other parts of the world live in fear
In an instant, bombs may drop
Shots fired
Bodies dropping on impact
So many are numb to these acts
Why is this behavior normal?
Why do they love feeding people lies?
The corrupt have rocked its constituents to sleep
Most are in a deep sleep and unable to think
The people have relinquished their power in the name of hate
They scream she is great, but the soil is talking
The laws are flawed
The rivers are overflowing
The dollar lacks stability

The people are broken
And as the riots increase, the elite will call on the police

When that fails, they will throw innocent people into jail
Then America will fail

Cold World

In a world colder than the North Pole
With moods unpredictable like climate change
I encourage you to have faith
Fast and pray
Look to the Most High for discernment and guidance
Pray for wisdom and peace
This world is moving towards darkness
Surround yourself with the righteous
Peace will decrease

Distorted Reality

Reality strikes like a thief in the night.
When did we lose our way?
Many long for the old days, but it's all faded memories of good times.
Now we just complain about the current state.
Hopelessness sets in like a face-lift.
So, we mask the current mental state with outburst, curse words, and disrespect.
Is it because they have controlled our intellect?
Programming my brown brothers into thinking that I am the enemy.
Or having the white middle class thinking they are better than me.
Their mind games have many focused on the game of life.
Living from check to check.
They've brainwashed people into becoming experts at playing checkers, while the elite play chess.
The reality is — the stage has been set.
We are puppets.
The government is the puppeteer pulling the strings.
They give people enough so they can barely survive but it's enough to pour into a system that doesn't see the people.
In fact, reality is distorted because so many think going backwards will make them great.
When you are brainwashed, you are unable to see hate.
So many yearn to be great at the expense of oppressing others.
They are willing to sacrifice their own wellbeing, just to worship demons.
Some are determined to do whatever it takes to make America great, even if it means their families live in poverty.

The Unknown

The day is near.
Sounds of explosions, people are scared.
Reality!
        Our worst fears are here.

Uncertainty

Battling for a place called home
Wanting to feel accepted by those that do not accept themselves
Struggling with sanity,
living life like it's vanity,
taking for granted the blessing of life.
Willing to pay any price for the meaningless things in life.
Unaware of the reality
gambling away every chance,
but hoping to not be another causality,
because in life there are always unexpected fatalities.

I'm Good

I don't want your reparations
the Most High has something more precious for me
I can't be bought or sold on your earthly possessions
keep that shit
I'm good
don't offer me your monopoly money, because it's acting funny
when the dollar crashes, toilet paper will be worth more than
your asses
you can keep your stolen land because the ground has spoiled
all your pesticides and experiments have ruined the soil
you have waged physical, mental, and spiritual war on my
community,
but I'm good
and now you want me to believe you come in peace
there is no peace when the world is on fire
systemic genocide because you want my people to die,
but I'm good
your lies have been exposed
with every truth told, you lie naked
bare to the bone
understand you cannot postpone what Abba will bestow upon you
so round of applause
come on
clap, clap, clap
your time is up
because what the Most High is about to reclaim no man can ever
takeaway
so, I'm good

I Love You

He said he loved me.
So, I opened my legs.
He showered me with the finest materials, so I gave him what was priceless.
I gave him time and my inner thoughts.
He gave me money.
I told him I loved him; he started acting funny.
I dialed him but the phone was busy.
I laid at night wondering where I went wrong.
I started playing those sad love songs.
Then I realized he was gone.
Damn, he walked away.
Now every encounter, I'm searching for his face.
So now I cherish what is priceless because the brother left me lifeless.
I haven't been the same ever since.
Sometimes, I reminisce on what I thought it could've been.
But I should've been thinking about what he presented to me.
Damn, he could've been the one, but he was the one that I should've allowed to walk away.
I understand I caught a stray that didn't know how to behave.

Representative

He came in peace,
Courted me with material things.
He kept my belly fat with the finest food.
He made love to me with his words.
He had me drunk and intoxicated by his touch.
I often blushed when he gazed into my eyes.
He had my heart dancing for joy.
He would whisper, "Don't be coy."
His scent had me high, so I decided to let him inside.
He held me tightly until I had fallen asleep.
I felt at peace.
I was in a deep sleep.
I woke up to a letter that said, "Read me."
I felt a profound sense of emptiness.
His words left me speechless.
His letter read.
           "Sheep,"
"For only one night."
"I hope you have a good life."

Sister to Sister

Carry my Crown,

Sometimes, I hurt inside. I may even show signs. Please don't tear me down because I don't smile. Don't add to my pain by misrepresenting my character, because our interactions have created misunderstandings. I've seen better days but today is not my day. I present a smile but internally it's a frown. My gown has been torn into pieces. My glow is dim. There's no light when I enter a room. Only emotionless stares with the look of fear. I may act as if I don't care, but deep down I'm hoping for an intervention. But I'm unwilling to allow you into a place where peace and safety no longer resides. Could it be pride? I can no longer hide the hurt. I often act out but it's not you, "It's me." So, I put up a wall no one can climb. Truth is I am flawed but you match my energy and now we're both moving envious. Backstabbing each other! Gossiping and spreading rumors. Dividing the people. I'm broken but searching for ways to make myself whole. I struggle to cope but I look at you and sometimes I see hope. But I may come off brash, so you give me your ass to kiss. Truth is we're just two Sisters navigate boardrooms, but these rooms give me the blues. I'm unable to overcome my demons, to allow me to win. Please understand this is no ordinary day. I'm just trying to find my way. But the battles make me afraid. You may feel threatened by me, but I just want to coexist in a world where Black women aren't condemned. I just want to see us win. Sis, today is not my day. I'm off my game, so I need you to carry my crown. Please don't let me down.

Sticks and Stones

the sticks don't hurt me
the words used, do not define me
learn not to try me

Tacos

the tacos were crunchy
see, I ate several for lunch
after I was done, I drank cherry punch

Dependable

Dependable
That is, You
Creator of all things
Nothing or no one will ever take Your place

When times are tough, I rely on my faith
When life seems hopeless, I look to You
Your love is correction
Your love is a blessing
Your protection is all I need to get by in life
Every day I rise, is the blessing of new life
I open my eyes and look at the sky, All Praises to the Most High

Dependable
That is, You
Creator of all things
Nothing or no one will ever take Your place

When I am sick, I rely on my faith
You restore my physical, spiritual and mental state to a healthy
state
Healer of my mind, body, and soul; that is why I never lose hope
You are my strength when I am weak
You are my mind when I need to think
You articulate the things I am unable to say
When I am sad or lonely,
You are right there to console me

Dependable
That is, You
Creator of all things
Nothing or no one will ever take Your place

What Does Your Love Look Like?

To know Your love is a blessing. The essence of Your beauty defines the love You have for Your children. You correct me when I am wrong. You love me through my mistakes. Your love strengthens my ability to endure the trials that come my way. Your love is the faith to believe in the things I cannot see. There is no limit to how much You have forgiven me. I keep Your commandments because that is the love You have given me. The calm before the storm. Your love is like a beautiful song. The comforter when things go wrong. The guidance on a journey filled with temptation. The force within my life, keeping me levelheaded. Your love gives me rest when I am weary or stressed. Your love helps me carry the burden. There is no greater love than Your love.

Wake Me

Wake me when the sun rises.
I want to see the mountain top.
Take me to the peak.
I'm confident you won't allow me to drop.
Guide me through the darkness.
Comfort me through the pain.
Spiritually cleanse me when it rains.
Shield me from the pain.
Give me the eyes to see the truth.
Open my ears to hear the word.
Walk with me throughout this journey.
Wrap your arms around me.
Endure with me until the end.

Rain

drizzle, drizzle,
boom, boom,
a storm is near
sirens,
warnings,
the smell of rain is in the air
the humidity thickens
the clock is ticking
the birds disappear in the gray skies
the forecast is cloudy
the thunderstorms are vibrant
feel the rain in the air
pouring, pouring,
the rainstorm is coming

Alone

I am not alone.
The journey has been tough.
The battles are never-ending.
Often, I have dreamed of winning.
Sometimes, I fall short.
Sometimes, I lose.
Sometimes, I have questioned the stops along the way.
Here I am today.
The feeling of loneliness seems empty.
The trials and casualties have missed me.
Sometimes, I need a hug.
Sometimes, I wonder where is the love.
Sometimes, I envision a place called peace.
Then reality hits me and loneliness kisses me.

You

Hi beautiful,
Turn that frown into a smile
As you beam, it lights up a room
You are loved by many
They admire your determination
Your journey is an inspiration to many
You are enough
You are the perfect destination
You bring joy to all
You are worthy of peace
You are worthy of love
Love yourself more than enough
You are unique
You deserve your flowers

All Right

I understand life is difficult. A lifetime of battle scars leaves so many broken beyond repair. The world has changed. The elders are resting peacefully. Distance has created strangers. Reunions are in danger. People struggle to cope with the reality of failure. Hold on, my brother. Be strong, my sister. Every day brings another challenge. I cannot guarantee life will be all right but keep fighting. No matter how difficult life gets, show up for yourself. Scream when you need to feel free. Cry for relief. This is a no judgment zone. This is a place called peace. You are safe with me. Know I am a call away. I will always be by your side. Lift you up when you stumble. Speak life when you need a lifeline. Your scars are mine. I will hold you close when it hurts. You can cry on my shoulder. Sis, have no fear. Bro, know that I care. It's going to be all right. I'll always be here.

Forgiveness

It takes courage to forgive
Forgiveness is necessary for you to be free
Freedom is a chance to survive
Forgiveness is a chance to thrive in ways you didn't know exist
Every day is the blessing of new life
The opportunity to be alive physically and spiritually, while
healing emotionally
Forgiveness is a new beginning that encourages healthy living
A chance to heal is the opportunity to restore what has been
broken
Never allow what has broken you to turn into what imprisons you,
keeping your mind, body and soul in bondage
It's not easy to forgive
Sometimes, forgiveness may be the hardest thing you have to do
Life is a journey filled with obstacles
Sometimes, you will experience good and bad times along the way
The choices you make will impact you every day
Choosing forgiveness takes back what was lost
The hurt that you feel is real
Don't allow the hurt to stop you from living
Forgiveness is for you
Start a new journey today by forgiving those who have hurt you
Forgiveness is hard but forgiveness allows you to be free to begin
the process of peace

She Is

She is phenomenal
An imperfect being navigating life's seasons
And with every season, she sees a side of herself she didn't know
exist
She possesses strength, which is a blessing
She was meticulously created with love and care
She is flawed but not easily broken
She is confident in her spirituality
She walks with grace
She embraces her femininity
She's intentional in all aspects of her life
Her faith is unmatched
There are moments when she is physically and mentally
exhausted, but she wears it well
Sometimes her crown may slide but her glory will always reside
She is the source of respect, dignity, empowerment and
motivation for other women
She may rise,
And she may fall but she never loses faith or sight of home
She is the embodiment of all things good
She is wisdom
She is powerful
She is earth
She is worthy
She is love
She is successful
She is you

Shine

It's your time to shine!
Endless possibilities await you
Dream big
Think positively
Speak life into your goals
Shoot for the stars
Have confidence in yourself
It's your time, opportunities await you
Make every moment count
Greatness is within you
Shine bright
You are a diamond

Cherish the Time

Here today, gone today. Time is not on our side. At any given moment your journey may come to an end. We take time for granted by procrastinating or delaying the things that matter, because we assume we have time. Truly we are all on borrowed time. Appreciate time because it is valuable. Once time has passed, we can no longer get it back. Pick up the phone and make peace, while they can speak. Reminisce about the times when precious memories were created. Smile about the time you laughed. Touch your heart and reflect about the times you cried. Value good and bad times. It's all valuable time. Naively, we think we have so much time until there's no time left. Hold those who matter closely. Love and appreciate those who are important. Within time life will transition to a physical ending but a time for spiritual beginnings. Cherish the time.

I Cried for You

Today, I cried for you.
I looked for a memory of you.
The pictures touched my soul.
The sound of your voice seems like a distant memory.
I miss you more than I can express.
Life hasn't been the same since you've left.
Today, I cried internally, because I was afraid to let anyone know I was struggling.
It's the little things that remind me of you.
Sometimes, the rain resembles your essence.
The sun reminds me of your warm embrace.
Winter days give me hope.
But today, I cried because I struggled to remember your voice.
The thought of never hearing your voice saddens me.
Sometimes, the days seem never-ending.
The thought of you not here hurts me physically.
Every night I dream of you.
The dreams reflect the time we spent together.
Every morning, I try to delay the inevitable with hopes of more time with you.
Reality is, I must let you go.
But I'm afraid the memories will fade away.

I Wanna

I wanna hold what I cannot feel
I wanna dream of you, but is it real?
I wanna sleep, so I'll be at peace
I wanna talk to you but the phone just rings
I wanna hear your voice just one more time
I wanna wake up one day and hope the thought of losing you
won't hurt so much inside
I wanna rewind time and go back to the day before we said
goodbye

It's so Hard to Say Goodbye

The day has come to say goodbye
My heart cries
I've hidden my tears
Seeing you has me crying uncontrollable tears
I long for one more time
Reality is, you are asleep
I miss the warmth of your touch
I yearn to look into your eyes and see life
Although your laughter is gone, I'll hold on to the memories we've
created
I pray for strength to cope with the difficulties of loss
I know you don't want me to mourn but it's hard
Seeing you lying here peacefully gives me hope
Dealing with loss is the hardest thing in life
I pray for comfort and time
The reality is not mine
The more I think about you, the more my heart sinks into further
extinction
But I know everything happens for a reason
Different storms
Different seasons
We all have a purpose
Some are here for a season
Others are here for several seasons
And even though it's so hard to say goodbye, I'm praying we meet
again on the other side
Until that time: farewell and good night

Mourning

I cried for you today
I hoped you would not walk away
I dreamed you were free
I prayed you were at peace

Grandma

The much-needed wing to keep her family afloat
The inspiration to keep her kin focused on being the best
The focal point of her family
Chosen
Leader
Nourisher
Nurturer
Thoughtful
Strength
The ground beneath her family's feet
Mother Nature
Mother Earth
Crowned since birth
Beautiful
Queen Bee
Selfless
Wisdom
Survivor
Powerful
She represents strength
A grandmother always finds a way to right the wrongs
She completes the family tree
Repairs the broken wings
Breathes life into dreams
There is no limit to the things she would do for her family
The world knows grandmothers are the truth

About the Author

TIKIA CLEMENT is an author, poet, and songwriter from the Bronx, New York. She began writing at the age of seven because of her love for music. Tikia found comfort in writing music and poetry in the bathroom. Writing in the bathroom became a part of her process of creating music and poetry. She took time away from writing to further her education in Human Resource Management. She has an M.S. in Business Administration with a concentration in Human Resource Management.

In 2021, Ms. Clement self-published her first poetry book, "Eye Am Poetry." In 2023, she released "Testifying My Way," her poetic dedication to the MOST HIGH. In addition, in 2024, she released "Shades of Emotions" and "Lift Up Your Voice." 2026 will be exciting for Tikia, as she will release a Poetry EP and Digital Journal.

Acknowledgements

I want to thank the MOST HIGH for giving me the courage and blessing me with the ability to share my poetry with the world.

In addition, I want to thank my family and friends for always being supportive.

Furthermore, I want to thank my editor for always doing a wonderful job and making sense of my words. Many thanks to my graphic designer, you always go above and beyond to create beautiful covers.

A Message from the Author

Every day is another blessing – another opportunity to give all the glory and praise to the MOST HIGH, for showing favor over you by giving you another chance to be the light and the best version of yourself.

Take care of your temple. Your health is the foundation of your mind, body and soul. Healthy living is invaluable. Take care of your mental, physical and spiritual health. Take this time to reflect and write three things you want to improve in your life. Consider what steps you need to take to make these improvements.

Empowering and motivating people is a gift and a blessing. Be the change and the good this world needs.

www.ingramcontent.com/pod-product-compliance
Lightning Source LLC
Chambersburg PA
CBHW020812130626
46554CB00006B/2395